SONJA T. A. LEKATOMPESSY

The Wear Rate of Zinc Anode on Surface Underwater of Ships

in Reducing Corrosion Rate

Department of Naval Architecture , Faculty of Technology, University of Pattimura, Jl.Ir. Putuhena No 1. Poka Ambon, Indonesia.

Corresponding author: sonja.lekatompessy@gmail.com

First edition

ISBN: 9798327872042

Editing by Andy Ismail

Contents

Acknowledgement

Thank to the Faculty of Engineering, Pattimura University as a funder (PNBP fund of the Faculty of Engineering in 2021) so that this research can be completed according to the set schedule.

Authorship

Sonja T. A. Lekatompessy[a]

[1]*Department of Naval Architecture , Faculty of Technology, University of Pattimura,*

Jl. Ir. Putuhena No 1. Poka Ambon, Indonesia

[a]Corresponding author: *sonja.lekatompessy@gmail.com*

Abstract

One way to reduce the rate of corrosion on the surface underwater area of the ship is to use Zink Anode. The wear rate is an important role in knowing how much Zink Anode can meet the needs of surface underwater area of hull plate to reduce of corrosion rate. This study aims to obtain protection against corrosion rate by conducting analysis of the wear rate on Zink Anodes in the field and calculation data so that the exact rate of use of Zink Anodes is installed according to the need to reduce the corrosion rate. To know the ability of Zink Anode installed, it takes corrosion rate data in the last 5 years from 3 ships and also the number of Zink Anodes used annually. As a result of this study, the wear rate that tends to remain and decrease can reduce the corrosion rate. Whereas, the increasing wear rate results in an increased corrosion rate.

Keywords: zinc anode, wear rate, corrosion rate, cathodic protection, ship hull.

Introduction

A ship's corrosion control includes steel materials, protective coatings, and cathodic protection, which should be considered in all stages of a ship's life. The protective coating is a primary element of corrosion control. Properly selected coating materials and application practices for these large and complex ships involve significant financial investments to achieve increased service life with minimum in-service maintenance and repairs, which, in turn, promotes the security of life and property and preservation of the natural environment [1].

A ship's corrosion control is a multifaceted endeavor that encompasses the selection of appropriate steel materials, the application of protective coatings, and the implementation of cathodic protection systems. These elements must be carefully considered throughout the entire lifespan of a vessel, from its initial design and construction to its operational life and eventual decommissioning. Among these, the protective coating plays a paramount role as the first line of defense against corrosion. The choice of coating materials and the methods employed for their application are critical, particularly for large and complex ships.

These decisions entail substantial financial investments, but they are essential for extending the service life of the vessel while minimizing the need for maintenance and repairs during its operation. By effectively managing corrosion, ship owners not only safeguard their investments but also contribute to the safety of the crew and cargo, protect valuable assets, and uphold environmental preservation by preventing the release of hazardous substances into the marine ecosystem.

An assessment of performance of zinc anodes on the cathodic protection of mild steel in 0.5 M hydrochloric acid was made at both the room and elevated temperatures. The cathodic protection reactions process was evaluated by weight-loss method, corrosion rate calculation and potential measurement methods. The effectiveness of zinc sacrificial anodes were found to be cathodically protective on mild steel in the hydrochloric acid at both the room temperature (27°C) and elevated temperature (60°C). There was close correlation of the results obtained for the weight-loss method and potential measurement in the HCL environment [2].

In a study by Cleophas et al. (2019), the performance of zinc anodes in protecting mild steel from corrosion in a 0.5 M hydrochloric acid (HCl) solution was assessed at both room temperature (27°C) and elevated temperature (60°C). The effectiveness of the cathodic protection provided by the zinc anodes was evaluated using weight-loss measurements, corrosion rate calculations, and potential measurements. The results demonstrated that the zinc anodes were effective in cathodically protecting the mild steel from corrosion in the HCl environment at both temperature levels. Furthermore, there was a strong correlation between the results obtained from the weight-loss method and potential measurements, indicating the reliability of these methods in assessing the performance of zinc anodes in this specific corrosive environment.

In order to minimize the risk of failures or major renewals of hull structures during the ship's expected life span, it is imperative that the precaution must be taken with regard to an adequate margin of safety against any one or combination of failure modes including excessive yielding, buckling, brittle fracture, fatigue and corrosion. The most efficient system for combating underwater corrosion is 'cathodic protection'. The basic principle of this method is that the ship's structure is made cathodic, i.e. the anodic (corrosion) reactions are suppressed by the application of an opposing current and the ship is there by protected [3].

To ensure the longevity and structural integrity of a ship's hull throughout its operational life, it is crucial to implement precautionary measures that address a wide range of potential failure modes. These failure modes encompass excessive yielding, buckling, brittle fracture, fatigue, and corrosion. Among these, corrosion poses a significant threat to the underwater portions of the hull. To mitigate this risk, cathodic protection has emerged as the most effective system for combating underwater corrosion. The fundamental principle behind cathodic protection involves rendering the ship's structure cathodic, effectively suppressing the anodic reactions that lead to corrosion. This is achieved by applying an opposing current, thereby safeguarding the ship from the detrimental effects of corrosion.

Development of mechanically rechargeable zinc-air batteries is discussed; attention is centered on anode- electrolyte composite since anodes are consumed during discharge, and qualitative tests conducted are destructive; performance tests have been made with 30 randomly selected samples representing lot size of 500 to 1000 anodes; anodes are tested against specification to determine if they meet physical, chemical, and electrical parameters, such as size, weight, amalgamation, absorbency, porosity, activated and unactivated storage, low temperature, and as battery assembly [4].

In the development of mechanically rechargeable zinc-air batteries, the anode-electrolyte composite is a focal point due to the consumption of anodes during discharge. The qualitative tests employed in this development process are destructive in nature. To assess performance, tests are conducted on 30 randomly selected anode samples, representing a lot size ranging from 500 to 1000 anodes. These anodes undergo rigorous testing against established specifications to ensure they meet various physical, chemical, and electrical parameters. These parameters include size, weight, amalgamation, absorbency, porosity, performance in both activated and unactivated storage conditions, low-temperature resilience, and overall functionality within a battery assembly.

Corrosion is one of the problems that is often encountered in the use of ferrous metal materials in everyday life both at home and industrial scale. Many methods for inhibiting the corrosion process in iron, one of which is by cathodic protection with a sacrificial method. The sacrificial material used contains more negative potential energy than iron. In this study AISI 1020 steel which will be protected with zinc as sacrificial anodel, which is assisted by AZ31 magnesium and aluminum 8011 additional metal. The testing process is carried out by the weight loss method, where the material is soaked for 2 months. The results showed no weight reduction in aluminum 8011, AISI 1020 steel and zinc when aluminum 8011 was added to this protection. But a weight reduction occurred in magnesium AZ3 1 when the magnesium was used as additional metal [5].

Corrosion, a prevalent issue affecting ferrous metals in both domestic and industrial settings, can be mitigated through various methods. One such method is cathodic protection, employing a sacrificial approach. This technique involves using a sacrificial material with a more negative potential energy than iron. Kusumaningrum and Usman (2019) conducted a study where AISI 1020 steel was protected using zinc as the sacrificial anode, supplemented by AZ31 magnesium and aluminum 8011 as additional metals. The weight loss method was employed to assess the effectiveness of this protection over a two-month immersion period. The results indicated that the addition of aluminum 8011 did not lead to any weight reduction in the aluminum, steel, or zinc. However, when magnesium AZ31 was used as an additional metal, a weight reduction was observed.

Corrosion of steel tube in sea water was controlled by cathodic protection. Sacrificial anode technique was used. In this technique, weight loss method was used to determine the rate of zinc consumption as a function of temperature, time, pH and solution velocity. Reaction kinetics studies showed that the rate of zinc consumption was first order. Activation parameters were obtained from Arrhenius equation and transition state equation. Two mathematical models were suggested to represent the consumption data. Statistical analysis proved that the second- order multi-terms model was better than the one-term model [6].

Yaro et al. (2013) investigated the corrosion control of steel tubes in seawater using cathodic protection with sacrificial zinc anodes. The weight loss method was employed to determine the rate of zinc consumption, examining its dependence on temperature, time, pH, and solution velocity. Reaction kinetics studies revealed that the zinc consumption rate followed a first-order reaction. Activation parameters were derived from the Arrhenius equation and transition state equation. The researchers proposed two mathematical models to represent the consumption data, and statistical analysis indicated that a second-order multi-term model provided a superior fit compared to a one-term model [6].

From the graphs of ZAP calculation results in accordance with the theory and results of ZAP usage on nine vessels, the results obtained are clear that the addition of ZAP surface area and weight increase of ZAP affects the decrease in corrosion rate[7].

Lekatompessy and Latuhihin (2021) found that increasing the surface area and weight of zinc anodes (ZAP) led to a decrease in the corrosion rate of nine vessels. This observation aligns with the theoretical expectation that a larger and heavier ZAP would offer enhanced protection against corrosion.

Literature Review

Corrosion Control Mechanisms in Ships

Corrosion control in ships involves a combination of strategies aimed at mitigating the degradation of metal components due to electrochemical reactions with the environment. The primary methods of corrosion control in ships include:

Material Selection: The choice of materials plays a fundamental role in corrosion prevention. Marine-grade steels with enhanced corrosion resistance, such as those alloyed with chromium, nickel, or molybdenum, are often preferred for hull construction. Additionally, the use of corrosion-resistant alloys like aluminum or copper-nickel for specific components can further enhance the ship's resilience to corrosion [3].

Ship hulls, being the primary structural component exposed to the harsh conditions of seawater, require materials with exceptional corrosion resistance. Marine-grade steels, specifically those alloyed with chromium, nickel, or molybdenum, are often favored for hull construction due to their enhanced ability to withstand the corrosive effects of seawater [3]. These alloying elements improve the steel's passive film stability, reducing its susceptibility to pitting and crevice corrosion.

Furthermore, the use of corrosion-resistant alloys extends beyond the hull structure. Components such as propellers, rudders, and seawater piping systems are often fabricated from materials like aluminum or copper-nickel alloys. Aluminum, known for its lightweight and high strength-to-weight ratio, forms a protective oxide layer that provides excellent corrosion resistance in seawater [3]. Copper-nickel alloys, on the other hand, offer superior resistance to biofouling, a significant concern in marine environments where the accumulation of marine organisms can accelerate corrosion [3].

The selection of materials for specific components is often a trade-off between corrosion resistance, mechanical properties, cost, and manufacturability. For instance, while titanium offers exceptional corrosion resistance, its high cost and difficulty in fabrication limit its widespread use in shipbuilding. In contrast, stainless steels, while less corrosion-resistant than titanium, are more affordable and easier to work with, making them a popular choice for many marine applications [3].

Protective Coatings: Protective coatings act as a barrier between the metal substrate and the corrosive environment. These coatings can be organic (e.g., paints, resins) or inorganic (e.g., zinc, aluminum). They function by preventing direct contact between the metal and corrosive agents like seawater, oxygen, and salts. The effectiveness of a coating depends on its adhesion, thickness, impermeability, and resistance to mechanical damage [1].

These coatings act as a physical barrier, effectively preventing direct contact between the metal substrate and corrosive agents such as seawater, oxygen, and salts [1]. The two main categories of protective coatings are organic and inorganic.

Organic coatings, typically composed of paints, resins, and polymers, offer a versatile and customizable solution for corrosion protection [1]. These coatings can be formulated to provide various properties, such as adhesion, flexibility, abrasion resistance, and color. They are commonly used as topcoats, providing aesthetic appeal and additional protection against weathering and UV radiation. However, organic coatings may have limitations in terms of long-term durability and resistance to harsh chemicals.

Inorganic coatings, on the other hand, are often based on metals like zinc or aluminum. These coatings offer excellent corrosion resistance due to their inherent electrochemical properties. For instance, zinc coatings provide sacrificial protection by corroding preferentially to the steel substrate, thus safeguarding the underlying metal. Aluminum coatings form a tenacious oxide layer that acts as a barrier against corrosive agents. Inorganic coatings are known for their longevity and resilience in harsh environments, making them ideal for protecting critical areas of a ship's structure [1].

The effectiveness of any protective coating hinges on several key factors. Firstly, proper surface preparation is crucial to ensure adequate adhesion of the coating to the substrate. This may involve cleaning, degreasing, and roughening the metal surface to create a strong bond. Secondly, the thickness of the coating plays a significant role in its barrier properties. Thicker coatings generally offer better protection but may also be more prone to cracking or peeling. Thirdly, the impermeability of the coating is essential for preventing the ingress of corrosive agents. Coatings with low permeability effectively block the passage of water, oxygen, and ions, thus inhibiting the corrosion process [1].

Finally, the coating's resistance to mechanical damage, such as abrasion, impact, and flexural stress, is critical for maintaining its protective function throughout the ship's operational life.

Cathodic Protection (CP): Cathodic protection is an electrochemical technique that involves making the ship's hull the cathode of an electrochemical cell. This is achieved by either using sacrificial anodes (typically made of zinc or aluminum) or impressed current systems. Sacrificial anodes corrode preferentially, protecting the hull, while impressed current systems apply an external current to counteract the corrosion process [2].

Cathodic protection (CP) is an electrochemical technique employed to safe-guard a ship's hull from corrosion. It operates on the principle of transforming the hull into the cathode of an electrochemical cell [2]. This can be achieved through two primary methods: sacrificial anodes or impressed current systems.

Sacrificial anodes, typically composed of zinc or aluminum, are electrically connected to the steel hull. Due to their more anodic (less noble) nature compared to steel, these anodes corrode preferentially. This sacrificial corrosion generates an electrical current that flows towards the steel hull, effectively suppressing the anodic reactions responsible for steel corrosion. In essence, the sacrificial anode acts as a "sacrificial lamb," corroding in place of the hull and thereby protecting it [2].

On the other hand, impressed current systems utilize an external power source to supply a direct current to the hull. This current counteracts the natural corrosion process by forcing electrons onto the hull, making it cathodic and inhibiting the anodic reactions that lead to corrosion. Impressed current systems offer greater flexibility and control compared to sacrificial anodes, as the current output can be adjusted to suit the specific requirements of the vessel and its operating environment [2].

Both sacrificial anodes and impressed current systems are effective methods of cathodic protection, each with its own advantages and disadvantages. Sacrificial anodes are relatively simple and inexpensive to install and maintain, but they have a limited lifespan and may not be suitable for large structures or highly corrosive environments. Impressed current systems, while more complex and costly, offer greater control and can be tailored to protect larger or more complex structures. The choice between the two methods depends on various factors, such as the size and type of vessel, the operating conditions, and the desired level of protection.

Design Considerations: Proper ship design can significantly influence corrosion control. This includes minimizing crevices and areas where water can accumulate, ensuring adequate ventilation to prevent moisture buildup, and selecting welding techniques that minimize residual stresses and promote uniform coating application [3].

Ship design plays a pivotal role in corrosion control strategies. A well-thought-out design can significantly reduce the vulnerability of a ship's structure to corrosion. One crucial aspect is minimizing crevices and areas where water can accumulate. These areas often become hotspots for corrosion due to the prolonged exposure to moisture and the formation of stagnant zones where oxygen concentration gradients can develop, leading to localized corrosion. By designing smooth surfaces and ensuring proper drainage, the risk of crevice corrosion and other forms of localized attack can be significantly reduced [3].

Adequate ventilation is another critical design consideration. Proper ventilation helps to prevent the buildup of moisture within the ship's structure, particularly in enclosed spaces such as tanks and cargo holds. High humidity levels can accelerate corrosion by providing a conducive environment for electrochemical reactions. By incorporating effective ventilation systems, ship designers can maintain a dry atmosphere within the ship, thereby inhibiting the onset and progression of corrosion [3].

The choice of welding techniques also influences corrosion control. Welding introduces residual stresses into the metal, which can make it more susceptible to stress corrosion cracking. By selecting welding techniques that minimize residual stresses, such as preheating and post-weld heat treatment, the risk of stress corrosion cracking can be reduced. Additionally, proper welding ensures uniform coating application, as inconsistencies in the weld profile can create areas where the coating is thinner or more prone to damage, leaving the underlying metal vulnerable to corrosion [3].

Maintenance and Inspection: Regular maintenance and inspection are essential for identifying and addressing corrosion issues early on. This includes cleaning the hull, repairing damaged coatings, and replacing sacrificial anodes as needed. Non-destructive testing techniques like ultrasonic thickness measurement can be used to assess the condition of the hull and detect hidden corrosion [1].

Regular maintenance and inspection are essential for identifying and addressing corrosion issues early on. This includes cleaning the hull to remove marine growth and debris, repairing any damaged coatings to maintain their protective barrier, and replacing sacrificial anodes as they deplete to ensure continued cathodic protection. Non-destructive testing (NDT) techniques, such as ultrasonic thickness measurement, play a crucial role in assessing the condition of the hull. By measuring the thickness of the hull plating, inspectors can detect areas of thinning caused by corrosion, even if they are not visible on the surface. This allows for timely repairs and prevents further degradation of the hull structure [1].

The effectiveness of corrosion control in ships depends on a holistic approach that considers all these factors. By integrating material selection, protective coatings, cathodic protection, design considerations, and regular maintenance, ship owners and operators can significantly extend the lifespan of their vessels, reduce maintenance costs, and ensure the safety and reliability of maritime operations.

In addition to these primary methods, several other factors influence corrosion control in ships. Environmental conditions, such as water temperature, salinity, and the presence of pollutants, can significantly affect the rate of corrosion. For instance, warmer waters tend to accelerate corrosion reactions, while higher salinity levels can increase the conductivity of the electrolyte, facilitating the electrochemical process [6].

Moreover, the ship's operational profile plays a crucial role. Ships operating in harsh environments, such as those exposed to ice or frequent contact with abrasive materials, may experience accelerated wear and tear on coatings, leading to increased vulnerability to corrosion. Similarly, vessels operating in areas with high levels of biological activity may be susceptible to microbiologically influenced corrosion (MIC), where microorganisms contribute to the degradation of metal surfaces [8].

To address these challenges, ship owners and operators often employ a combination of corrosion control methods. For example, a ship's hull may be coated with a multi-layered system consisting of a primer, an intermediate coat, and a topcoat, each designed to provide specific protective properties. Additionally, sacrificial anodes may be strategically placed on the hull to provide cathodic protection, while impressed current systems may be used for larger vessels or those operating in highly corrosive environments.

Furthermore, advancements in technology have led to the development of new corrosion control solutions. These include the use of smart coatings that can self-heal when damaged, as well as the application of nanotechnology to create more durable and effective protective layers. The integration of sensors and monitoring systems allows for real-time assessment of the ship's condition, enabling proactive maintenance and repair before corrosion becomes a significant problem.

Zinc Anodes as Sacrificial Protection

Zinc anodes are widely used as sacrificial anodes in cathodic protection systems for ships. The principle behind their operation is based on the galvanic series, which ranks metals according to their electrochemical reactivity [2]. Zinc, being more anodic (less noble) than steel, will corrode preferentially when electrically connected to the steel hull. This sacrificial corrosion of the zinc anode generates an electrical current that flows to the steel, suppressing the anodic reactions responsible for steel corrosion and thus protecting the hull [2].

The effectiveness of zinc anodes as sacrificial protection depends on several factors, including the size and shape of the anode, the composition of the seawater, the temperature, and the presence of other metals in the system. Larger anodes have a greater capacity to provide protection, while higher temperatures and salinities generally accelerate the corrosion process, requiring more frequent anode replacement [6].

The composition of the zinc anode itself can also influence its performance. High-purity zinc anodes are typically preferred due to their consistent corrosion behavior and longer lifespan. Alloying elements like aluminum or cadmium can be added to improve specific properties, such as the anode's mechanical strength or its ability to function in cold water [4].

In addition to their use in protecting ship hulls, zinc anodes are also commonly employed in other marine structures, such as offshore platforms, pipelines, and harbor installations. Their versatility, effectiveness, and relative low cost make them a popular choice for cathodic protection in a wide range of marine applications. However, the proper selection, installation, and maintenance of zinc anodes are crucial to ensure their optimal performance and maximize the protection they offer against corrosion [7].

The performance of zinc anodes can be influenced by environmental factors and operational conditions. For instance, in highly corrosive environments, such as those with high salinity or temperatures, the wear rate of zinc anodes can increase, necessitating more frequent replacement [6]. Additionally, the presence of calcareous deposits or biofouling on the anode surface can hinder its effectiveness by reducing the exposed surface area and impeding the flow of current [8].

To optimize the performance of zinc anodes, various strategies can be employed. One approach is to use anodes with a larger surface area or to increase the number of anodes installed on the hull. This can provide a greater capacity for sacrificial corrosion and extend the time between anode replacements [7]. Another strategy is to use anodes with a higher purity of zinc, as these tend to corrode more uniformly and predictably.

Furthermore, the development of new anode materials and designs is an ongoing area of research. For example, some studies have explored the use of zinc alloys with improved corrosion resistance or the incorporation of additives that can enhance the anode's performance in specific environments. Additionally, the use of smart anodes equipped with sensors can provide real-time data on the anode's condition, allowing for more efficient maintenance and replacement schedules [4].

zinc anodes offering a reliable and cost-effective method for mitigating corrosion. Understanding the factors that influence their performance and implementing strategies to optimize their use are essential for ensuring the longevity and safety of marine vessels.

Factors Affecting Zinc Anode Wear Rate

Several factors influence the wear rate of zinc anodes, which, in turn, affects their lifespan and the effectiveness of cathodic protection systems.

Current Density: The rate at which zinc corrodes is directly proportional to the current density flowing through the anode. Higher current densities lead to faster consumption of the anode material, resulting in a shorter lifespan. The current density is influenced by the size and shape of the anode, the resistivity of the electrolyte (seawater), and the distance between the anode and the protected structure [6].

Current density, defined as the electrical current per unit area of the anode, is a critical factor influencing the rate of zinc anode corrosion. The relationship between current density and corrosion rate is directly proportional, meaning that as the current density increases, so does the rate at which the zinc anode is consumed [6]. This phenomenon can be attributed to the accelerated electrochemical reactions occurring at the anode surface when a higher current is applied. Consequently, higher current densities lead to a faster depletion of the anode material, resulting in a reduced lifespan and necessitating more frequent replacements.

Several factors contribute to the current density experienced by a zinc anode. The size and shape of the anode play a significant role, as a larger surface area allows for a more distributed current flow, reducing the current density at any given point. Conversely, smaller anodes or those with irregular shapes may experience localized areas of high current density, leading to accelerated corrosion in those regions [6].

The resistivity of the electrolyte, in this case, seawater, also influences the current density. Seawater with higher salinity levels exhibits lower resistivity, facilitating the flow of electrical current and potentially increasing the current density at the anode surface. Additionally, the distance between the anode and the protected structure affects the current density. Anodes placed closer to the hull will experience a higher current density compared to those located farther away, as the electrical resistance of the electrolyte decreases with proximity [6].

By carefully considering the size and shape of the anode, the salinity of the operating environment, and the distance between the anode and the protected structure, engineers can tailor the current density to achieve the desired level of protection while minimizing anode consumption and maximizing its lifespan.

Temperature: Elevated temperatures accelerate the corrosion process, leading to increased zinc anode consumption. This is due to the higher kinetic energy of the ions involved in the electrochemical reactions, which increases the rate of both anodic and cathodic reactions [6].

Elevated temperatures accelerate the corrosion process, leading to increased zinc anode consumption [6]. This phenomenon can be attributed to the fundamental principles of chemical kinetics. As temperature rises, the kinetic energy of the ions involved in the electrochemical reactions increases. This heightened energy facilitates the movement of ions, enhancing the rate of both anodic and cathodic reactions. In the context of zinc anodes, this means that the zinc atoms lose electrons more readily at the anode, while the reduction of oxygen or hydrogen ions at the cathode also occurs more rapidly. Consequently, the overall corrosion process is accelerated, leading to faster consumption of the zinc anode material.

This temperature dependence has significant implications for the design and maintenance of cathodic protection systems. In warmer waters, such as those found in tropical regions, zinc anodes may deplete more quickly, necessitating more frequent inspections and replacements to maintain adequate protection. Conversely, in colder environments, the rate of anode consumption may be slower, allowing for longer intervals between replacements. Understanding the impact of temperature on zinc anode performance is crucial for optimizing the effectiveness and cost-efficiency of cathodic protection systems in diverse marine environments.

Salinity: The salinity of seawater plays a significant role in the wear rate of zinc anodes. Higher salinity levels increase the conductivity of the electrolyte, facilitating the flow of current and accelerating the corrosion process. This is why ships operating in more saline waters, such as those in tropical regions, may require more frequent anode replacement [6].

Higher salinity levels correspond to an increased concentration of dissolved salts in the water, which in turn enhances the electrical conductivity of the electrolyte [6]. This heightened conductivity facilitates the flow of electrical current between the anode and the protected metal surface, accelerating the electrochemical reactions responsible for corrosion. As a result, zinc anodes immersed in more saline waters experience a faster rate of consumption due to the increased current flow.

This relationship between salinity and anode wear rate has practical implications for the maintenance of cathodic protection systems. Ships operating in regions with higher salinity levels, such as tropical waters, will generally require more frequent replacement of their zinc anodes compared to those operating in less saline environments [6]. This is because the accelerated corrosion rate in high-salinity conditions necessitates a greater sacrificial capacity to maintain adequate protection of the hull. Therefore, understanding the impact of salinity on zinc anode performance is essential for tailoring maintenance schedules and ensuring the long-term effectiveness of cathodic protection systems in varying marine environments.

Water Flow: The flow of water over the anode surface can affect its wear rate. High flow rates can remove corrosion products from the anode surface, exposing fresh zinc and increasing the rate of consumption. Conversely, stagnant water can lead to the buildup of calcareous deposits, which can hinder the anode's performance by reducing its effective surface area [8].

High flow rates can accelerate the anode's consumption by continuously removing the corrosion products that form on its surface. These corrosion products, typically zinc oxide and hydroxide, can act as a partial barrier, slowing down the corrosion process. However, when high flow rates are present, these protective layers are constantly swept away, exposing fresh zinc to the corrosive environment and increasing the rate at which it is consumed [8].

Conversely, in stagnant or low-flow conditions, the corrosion products are not effectively removed from the anode surface. Over time, these products can accumulate and form calcareous deposits, which are essentially layers of calcium carbonate and other minerals. These deposits can significantly hinder the anode's performance by reducing its effective surface area, thus limiting the amount of zinc available for sacrificial corrosion [8]. Moreover, calcareous deposits can act as an insulating layer, impeding the flow of electrical current between the anode and the protected structure, thereby compromising the effectiveness of the cathodic protection system.

Therefore, the flow rate of water over the zinc anode surface presents a trade-off. While high flow rates can enhance the anode's initial performance by removing corrosion products, they can also lead to faster consumption and a shorter lifespan. On the other hand, low flow rates may promote the formation of calcareous deposits, which can hinder the anode's long-term effectiveness. Understanding this dynamic is crucial for optimizing the placement and design of zinc anodes in cathodic protection systems, ensuring a balance between efficient corrosion protection and anode longevity.

Anode Composition and Purity: The composition and purity of the zinc anode can significantly influence its wear rate. High-purity zinc anodes tend to corrode more uniformly and predictably, resulting in a longer lifespan. The presence of impurities or alloying elements can affect the anode's electrochemical behavior and may lead to uneven corrosion or premature failure [4].

The composition and purity of a zinc anode are pivotal in determining its wear rate and overall effectiveness. High-purity zinc anodes, characterized by a minimal presence of impurities, exhibit a more uniform and predictable corrosion pattern, contributing to an extended operational lifespan [4]. This uniformity stems from the consistent electrochemical behavior of high-purity zinc, ensuring that the sacrificial corrosion process occurs evenly across the anode's surface.

Conversely, the presence of impurities or alloying elements within the zinc anode can significantly alter its electrochemical properties. These impurities can act as sites for localized corrosion, leading to uneven wear and potentially premature failure of the anode [4]. For instance, the presence of iron or other less noble metals can create micro-galvanic cells within the anode, accelerating the corrosion of the zinc in those specific areas. Similarly, alloying elements, while sometimes added to improve certain properties like mechanical strength, can also introduce variations in the anode's electrochemical potential, leading to non-uniform corrosion.

Therefore, the selection of zinc anodes for cathodic protection systems should prioritize high-purity zinc to ensure optimal performance and longevity. While alloyed anodes may offer specific advantages in certain applications, their potential for uneven corrosion and reduced lifespan should be carefully considered. By understanding the impact of composition and purity on zinc anode behavior, engineers and operators can make informed decisions to maximize the effectiveness and efficiency of cathodic protection systems.

Understanding these factors is crucial for predicting the lifespan of zinc anodes and optimizing their use in cathodic protection systems. By carefully considering the environmental conditions and operational parameters, engineers can select the appropriate anode type, size, and placement to ensure effective and long-lasting corrosion protection for marine structures.

In addition to the factors mentioned previously, several other variables can influence the wear rate of zinc anodes. The presence of other metals in the system, such as copper or stainless steel, can create galvanic couples with the zinc anode, accelerating its corrosion. This is because zinc is more anodic than these metals, and in a galvanic couple, the more anodic metal corrodes preferentially [5].

The design and configuration of the cathodic protection system also play a role. For example, the spacing and distribution of anodes on the hull can affect the uniformity of current distribution, which in turn influences the wear rate of individual anodes. Improper anode placement can lead to uneven current distribution, causing some anodes to wear out faster than others [7].

Furthermore, the presence of calcareous deposits or biofouling on the anode surface can significantly impact its wear rate. These deposits can act as a barrier, reducing the effective surface area of the anode and hindering the flow of current. This can lead to localized corrosion and premature failure of the anode [8].

To mitigate these effects, regular maintenance and inspection of the cathodic protection system are crucial. This includes cleaning the anodes to remove deposits, monitoring their condition, and replacing them as needed. Additionally, the use of antifouling coatings on the anodes can help prevent the accumulation of biofouling and ensure their optimal performance.

The wear rate of zinc anodes is a complex phenomenon influenced by a multitude of factors. Understanding these factors and their interactions is essential for designing and maintaining effective cathodic protection systems for ships and other marine structures. By carefully considering the environmental conditions, operational parameters, and system design, engineers can optimize the use of zinc anodes to ensure long-lasting and reliable corrosion protection.

Measuring and Predicting Corrosion Rates

Accurately measuring and predicting corrosion rates is essential for effective corrosion control in ships. Several methods are commonly employed to assess the extent and rate of corrosion on ship hulls and other marine structures:

Weight Loss Method: This is a straightforward method that involves measuring the weight of a metal sample before and after exposure to a corrosive environment. The difference in weight represents the amount of metal lost due to corrosion. By dividing the weight loss by the exposure time and surface area of the sample, the corrosion rate can be calculated. This method is simple and inexpensive but may not be suitable for in-situ measurements on large structures [8].

The weight loss method is a simple and cost-effective technique used to quantify corrosion rates. It involves measuring the weight of a metal sample before and after exposure to a corrosive environment, such as seawater. The difference in weight directly corresponds to the amount of metal lost due to corrosion [8]. By dividing this weight loss by the exposure time and the surface area of the sample, the corrosion rate can be calculated, typically expressed in millimeters per year (mm/year). This method is particularly useful for laboratory experiments and for assessing the corrosion resistance of different materials under controlled conditions. However, its applicability for in-situ measurements on large structures, like ship hulls, is limited due to the impracticality of removing and weighing large sections of the structure [8].

Corrosion Coupons: Corrosion coupons are small metal samples of known dimensions that are intentionally exposed to the corrosive environment alongside the structure being monitored. By periodically retrieving and analyzing these coupons, engineers can assess the corrosion rate and the effectiveness of the corrosion control measures in place.

Corrosion coupons are small metal samples with precisely known dimensions that are strategically placed within the corrosive environment alongside the structure being monitored. These coupons serve as sacrificial indicators of the corrosive conditions present. By periodically retrieving and analyzing these coupons, engineers can gain valuable insights into the rate of corrosion and the effectiveness of the implemented corrosion control measures. The analysis of corrosion coupons typically involves measuring their weight loss, examining their surface for signs of corrosion, and conducting electrochemical tests to determine the corrosion rate. This information allows engineers to assess the performance of protective coatings, cathodic protection systems, and other corrosion control strategies, enabling them to make informed decisions regarding maintenance, repair, and replacement of components.

Linear Polarization Resistance (LPR): LPR is an electrochemical technique that measures the polarization resistance of a metal surface, which is inversely proportional to the corrosion rate. This method can provide real-time corrosion rate data and is suitable for in-situ measurements on large structures. However, it requires specialized equipment and expertise.

Linear Polarization Resistance (LPR) is an electrochemical technique used to measure the polarization resistance of a metal surface. This polarization resistance is inversely proportional to the corrosion rate, meaning that a higher polarization resistance indicates a lower corrosion rate. LPR is a valuable tool for real-time monitoring of corrosion rates and is particularly suitable for in-situ measurements on large structures like ship hulls. However, the successful application of LPR requires specialized equipment and expertise to accurately interpret the data and derive meaningful corrosion rate values.

Electrochemical Impedance Spectroscopy (EIS): EIS is another electrochemical technique that measures the impedance of a metal surface over a range of frequencies. The resulting impedance spectrum can be analyzed to determine the corrosion rate and other electrochemical parameters. EIS is a powerful tool for investigating the mechanisms of corrosion and assessing the effectiveness of different corrosion control measures.

Electrochemical Impedance Spectroscopy (EIS) is a sophisticated electrochemical technique that measures the impedance (resistance to the flow of alternating current) of a metal surface across a wide range of frequencies. The resulting impedance spectrum, a plot of impedance against frequency, provides valuable information about the corrosion processes occurring at the metal-electrolyte interface. By analyzing the shape and characteristics of the impedance spectrum, engineers can determine the corrosion rate, as well as other important electrochemical parameters such as the double-layer capacitance, charge transfer resistance, and diffusion impedance. EIS is a powerful tool for investigating the mechanisms of corrosion, identifying the types of corrosion present, and evaluating the effectiveness of various corrosion control measures.

Ultrasonic Thickness Measurement (UTM): UTM is a non-destructive testing technique that uses ultrasonic waves to measure the thickness of a metal structure. By comparing the thickness measurements over time, engineers can detect and quantify the amount of metal lost due to corrosion. This method is particularly useful for assessing the condition of ship hulls and other large structures.

Ultrasonic Thickness Measurement (UTM) is a non-destructive testing technique that utilizes ultrasonic waves to gauge the thickness of metal structures. By comparing thickness measurements taken over time, engineers can identify and quantify the extent of metal loss due to corrosion. This method is particularly valuable for assessing the condition of large structures like ship hulls, as it allows for the detection of corrosion-induced thinning even in areas that are not easily accessible for visual inspection [8].

In addition to these techniques, several other methods can be employed to measure and predict corrosion rates in ships. These include:

1. **Visual Inspection:** While not a quantitative method, visual inspection is a crucial first step in assessing the condition of a ship's hull and identifying areas of concern. Experienced inspectors can identify signs of corrosion, such as rust, pitting, or cracking, and recommend appropriate action.

2. **Radiography:** Radiography can be used to detect internal corrosion that may not be visible on the surface. This technique involves passing X-rays or gamma rays through the metal structure and capturing the resulting image on film or a digital detector. Variations in the intensity of the radiation passing through the metal can reveal the presence of voids, cracks, or other defects caused by corrosion.

3. **Eddy Current Testing:** Eddy current testing is a non-destructive technique that uses electromagnetic induction to detect surface and near-surface flaws in conductive materials. By analyzing the changes in the eddy currents induced in the metal, inspectors can identify areas of corrosion or thinning.

4. **Statistical Modeling:** Statistical models can be developed based on

historical data and operational parameters to predict the expected corrosion rate of a ship's hull. These models can take into account factors such as the ship's age, operating environment, maintenance history, and the effectiveness of the corrosion control measures in place.

By combining these various measurement and prediction techniques, ship owners and operators can gain a comprehensive understanding of the corrosion status of their vessels. This information is crucial for making informed decisions regarding maintenance, repair, and replacement of components, ultimately ensuring the safety, reliability, and longevity of the ship.

The Modeling of Zinc Anode Consumption

One such model is the one proposed by Yaro et al. (2013), who developed a second-order multi-term model to represent the consumption data of zinc anodes in seawater. Their model considered the effects of temperature, time, pH, and solution velocity on the consumption rate. The statistical analysis showed that this model provided a better fit to the experimental data compared to a simpler one-term model, indicating its potential for accurate prediction of zinc anode consumption in real-world conditions [6].

Another approach to modeling zinc anode consumption involves the use of numerical simulations. These simulations can take into account the complex geometry of the anode and the protected structure, as well as the non-uniform distribution of current density. By solving the governing equations of electrochemistry and fluid dynamics, numerical simulations can provide detailed insights into the corrosion process and the consumption of zinc anodes.

The development of accurate and reliable models for zinc anode consumption is an ongoing research area. As technology advances, researchers are incorporating more sophisticated techniques, such as machine learning and artificial intelligence, to improve the predictive capabilities of these models.

This ongoing research is essential for optimizing the design and operation of cathodic protection systems, ensuring the long-term protection of marine structures from corrosion.

The second-order multi-term model developed by Yaro et al. (2013) is a significant advancement in predicting zinc anode consumption. This model incorporates the effects of temperature, time, pH, and solution velocity, providing a more comprehensive understanding of the factors influencing anode wear. The model's superior fit to experimental data compared to simpler models highlights its potential for accurate prediction in real-world scenarios, where these factors can vary significantly.

In addition to analytical models, numerical simulations offer a powerful tool for understanding zinc anode consumption. These simulations can account for the complex geometries of anodes and protected structures, as well as the non-uniform distribution of current density, which are often oversimplified in analytical models. By solving the governing equations of electrochemistry and fluid dynamics, numerical simulations can provide detailed insights into the corrosion process and the spatial distribution of anode consumption. This information is invaluable for optimizing the design and placement of anodes to ensure uniform protection and maximize their lifespan.

The development of accurate and reliable models for zinc anode consumption remains an active area of research. As technology advances, researchers are exploring the integration of more sophisticated techniques, such as machine learning and artificial intelligence, into these models. Machine learning algorithms can analyze large datasets of experimental and field data to identify patterns and relationships that may not be apparent through traditional modeling approaches. Artificial intelligence can be used to optimize the design of cathodic protection systems by considering a wide range of variables and constraints. These advancements in modeling techniques hold the promise of further improving the accuracy and reliability of zinc anode consumption predictions, ultimately leading to more effective and efficient corrosion control strategies for marine structures.

Methodology

Data collection is done by interview. Analysis of the wear rate on Zink Anodes in the field and calculation data so that the exact rate of use of Zink Anodes is installed according to the need to reduce the corrosion rate. To know the ability of Zink Anode installed, it takes corrosion rate data in the last 5 years from 3 ships and also the number of Zink Anodes used annually.

Weight loss measurement is a method used to calculate the difference between the initial weight and the final weight of the plate samples. According to weight loss method is a simply way to find out the performance of corrosion process of metal. The weight loss of the plate samples can be determined by using this mathemat ical Equation 1 [8]:

$$W_L = \omega_0 - \omega_1 \quad (1)$$

Where:

ω_0 = initial weight

ω_1 = final weight

W_L = weight loss

In order to obtain weight loss percentage, another mathematical Equation 2 [8]:

$$\text{Weight loss (\%)} = 100(1 - \omega 0 / \omega 1) \quad (2)$$

Where:

ω_0 = initial weight

ω_1 = final weight

W = Weight loss (%)

To obtain corroded plate weight data by changing the reduction of plate thickness (mm) each year into weight loss (gr) size to obtain corrosion rate from the following equation 3 [8]:

$$C_R = 87{,}6 \; x \; \left(\frac{W}{DAT}\right) \quad (3)$$

Where:

W = mass lost due to corroded (mg)

D = mass meeting (gr/cm^3)

= 7.8 mgr/m^3 or 490lb/ft^3

A = surface area (in^2)

T = test length (days)

In this research endeavor, the primary method of data collection involved conducting interviews. These interviews served as a valuable tool for gathering both qualitative and quantitative data related to the wear rate of zinc anodes and the corresponding corrosion rates on ship hulls. The interviews were strategically designed to target key personnel involved in the maintenance and operation of ships, such as crew members, engineers, and ship owners. These individuals possess firsthand knowledge and experience regarding the installation, inspection, and replacement of zinc anodes, as well as the observed corrosion patterns on the ship hulls.

The interview questions were structured to elicit specific information regarding the wear rate of zinc anodes over time. This involved inquiring about the number of anodes installed, the frequency of anode replacement, and any observed changes in the size or condition of the anodes. Additionally, the interviews sought to gather data on the corrosion rates of the ship hulls, including the methods used to measure corrosion, the frequency of inspections, and any historical records of corrosion incidents.

To complement the interview data, this study also incorporated field measurements and calculations. Field measurements involved the physical inspection of zinc anodes on selected ships to assess their wear and tear. This provided valuable visual evidence of the anode condition and allowed for the estimation of the remaining lifespan of the anodes. Furthermore, calculations were performed based on the collected data to determine the wear rate of zinc anodes and to correlate it with the observed corrosion rates.

The data obtained from interviews, field measurements, and calculations were then subjected to rigorous analysis. Statistical methods were employed to identify trends and patterns in the data, such as the relationship between anode wear rate and corrosion rate, as well as the influence of various factors on anode performance. The analysis aimed to provide a comprehensive understanding of the dynamics of zinc anode wear and its impact on corrosion control in ships.

By integrating data from diverse sources and employing a multi-faceted approach, this research sought to provide a comprehensive and reliable assessment of the wear rate of zinc anodes and its correlation with corrosion rates in ships. The findings of this study have significant implications for optimizing the use of zinc anodes in cathodic protection systems, ultimately contributing to the development of more effective and efficient corrosion control strategies in the maritime industry.

Results and Dicussion

The wear rate can be seen in Table 1, Table 2, and Table 3.

TABLE 1. All Zinc Anodes Installed Flow Rate

(Columns 1 through 10)

No	1 x 6	2 x 7	3 x 8	4 x 9	5 x 10	1 x 11	2 x 12	3 x 13	4 x 14	5 x 15	16A x 1
1	20.304	20.304	20.304	20.288	20.288	28.296	28.296	28.296	37.312	37.312	48.600
2	16.492	16.492	16.464	16.468	16.468	13.908	13.908	17.136	20.332	20.332	30.400
3	15.012	15.012	15.012	15.012	14.964	33.588	33.588	33.588	33.588	37.236	48.600

Description:

- Column 1 to column 5 = Wear rate total zinc anodes from the first year to the fifth year (m^3) 10^{-3}
- Column 6 to column 10 = Volume of total zinc anodes from the first year to the fifth year (m^3) 10^{-3}
- Column 11 = Volume of zinc anodes before the first year used (m^3)

Table 1 presents the wear rate and volume of zinc anodes installed on three ships over five years. The wear rate, representing the amount of zinc anode material lost due to corrosion, is given in cubic meters (m3) multiplied by

10^{-3}. The volume of zinc anodes, also in cubic meters multiplied by 10^{-3}, indicates the total volume of anodes installed on each ship each year. For instance, ship No. 1 had a wear rate of 20.304 m3 x 10^{-3} in the first year, with a total anode volume of 28.296 m3 x 10^{-3} in the sixth year. The table also includes the initial volume of zinc anodes before the first year of use, denoted as "Volume" in column 11.

TABLE 2. The Wear Rate per Zinc Anode (m3) x 103

No	YEAR I	YEAR II	YEAR III	YEAR IV	YEAR V
1	0.376	0.376	0.376	0.317	0.317
2	0.217	0.217	0.196	0.179	0.179
3	0.278	0.278	0.278	0.278	0.258

Table 2 illustrates the wear rate per zinc anode over five years, measured in cubic meters (m3) multiplied by 10^{-3}. In the first year, the wear rate for ship No. 1 was 0.376 m3 x 10^{-3}, while for ships No. 2 and 3, it was 0.217 m3 x 10^{-3} and 0.278 m3 x 10^{-3}, respectively. Over the five-year period, the wear rate for ship No. 1 remained constant, while it decreased slightly for ships No. 2 and 3. This suggests that the rate of zinc anode consumption varied among the ships and, in some cases, decreased over time, potentially indicating a decrease in the demand for cathodic protection.

TABLE 3. Zinc Anode Volume Remaining per Year

No	YEAR I	YEAR II	YEAR III	YEAR IV	YEAR V	VOLUME
1	0.524	0.524	0.524	0.583	0.583	0.900
2	0.183	0.183	0.204	0.221	0.221	0.400
3	0.622	0.612	0.622	0.622	0.642	0.900

Description:

- Zinc anode volume remaining per year is obtained by looking at the difference = a zinc anode – the wear rate (m^3) x 10^{-3})

Table 3 displays the volume of zinc anode remaining per year, also in cubic meters multiplied by 10^{-3}. In the first year, ship No. 1 had 0.524 m3 x 10^{-3} of zinc anode remaining, while ships No. 2 and 3 had 0.183 m3 x 10^{-3} and 0.612 m3 x 10^{-3} remaining, respectively. The volume of zinc anode remaining fluctuated slightly over the five-year period for all three ships. This fluctuation could be due to the varying wear rates and the addition of new anodes throughout the study period. The initial volume of the zinc anodes is also presented in this table.

Correlation Wear Rate of hull of ship on Corrosion Rate

The analysis was conducted on ships, each of which was made in its own analysis with attention to the problems reviewed. The three vessels reviewed, only a few ships will be featured in the correlation graph that occurs on the wear rate remaining between the theoretical wear rate and the wear rate installed in relation to corrosion rate.

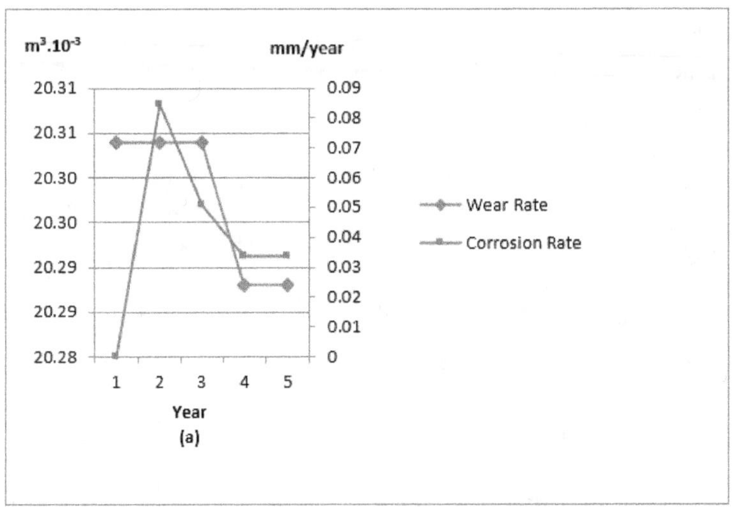

Figure 1. *Wear Rate and Corrosion Rate Correlation on Ship No. 1*

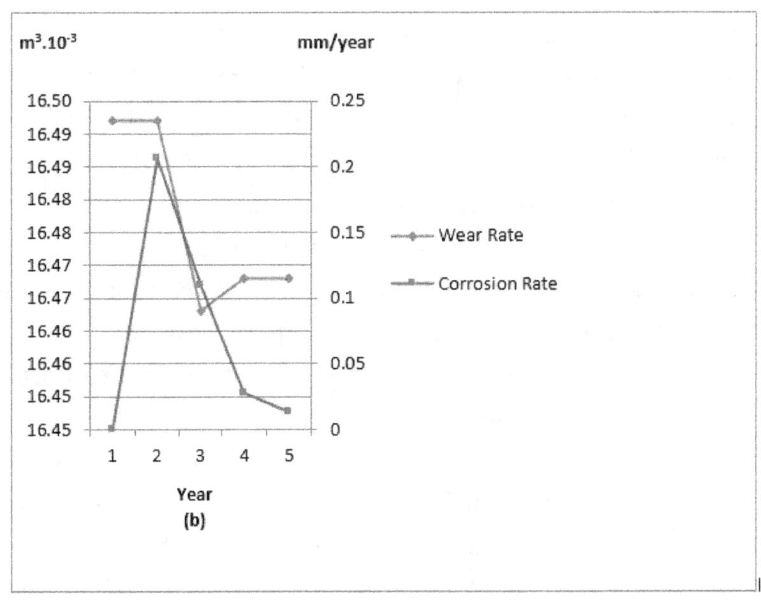

Figure 2. *Wear Rate and Corrosion Rate Correlation on Ship No. 2*

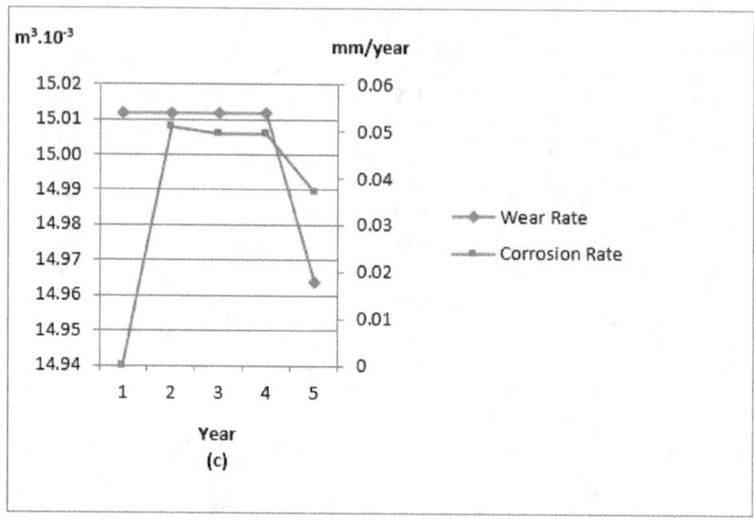

Figure 3. *Wear Rate and Corrosion Rate Correlation on Ship No.3*

In Figure 1, there was decrease the wear rate in the 3rd year to 20.30 m^3.10^3 and there was decrease corrosion rate in the 4th year to 0.0339 mm/year, this is due to the addition of zinc anode in that year. This shows that the needs of zinc anode have been sufficient for ship number 1. In Figure 2, until the 3rd year there was decrease in the wear rate to 16.46 m^3.10^3, in the 4th year there was increase to 16.47 m^3.10^3, Nevertheless, the rate of corrosion continued to decrease until the 5th year by 0.0138 mm /year. This indicates that the needs of zinc anode have been enough on the 2nd ship. On vessel No. 4, in the 3rd year the number of zinc anodes was increased and there was a reduction in corrosion rate close to normal.

With the addition of ZAP, it can be seen from figure 3 above that there was a decrease in corrosion rate in the 4th and 5th years where there was no significant corrosion of 0.0138 mm/year. In Figure 3, until the 4th year the wear rate of steady is 15.01 m^3.10^{-3}, the corrosion rate tends to remain at 0.0495 mm/year. In the 5th year there was an increase in zinc anode, this greatly affected the decrease in the rate of salting to 15.96 m^3.10^{-3}, as well as a decrease in corrosion rate to reach 0.0371 mm/year.

The analysis of zinc anode wear rates and their correlation with corrosion rates across nine vessels reveals intriguing insights. Vessels No. 2, 3, and 4 exhibited a clear trend: an increase in the total surface area of zinc anodes (ZAP) correlated with a decrease in the hull's corrosion rate.

For instance, in vessel No. 2, the addition of 10 more zinc anodes led to a substantial reduction in the corrosion rate, dropping from 0.0059 mm/year in the third year to 0.0339 mm/year in the fourth and fifth years. This observation suggests that the increased anode surface area provided enhanced cathodic protection, effectively mitigating the corrosion process.

A similar pattern emerged in vessel No. 3, where the addition of zinc anodes resulted in a decrease in the corrosion rate to a negligible 0.0138 mm/year in the fourth and fifth years. This finding further supports the notion that a larger anode surface area can significantly contribute to reducing corrosion rates.

Vessel No. 4 also demonstrated this trend. After increasing the number of zinc anodes in the third year, the corrosion rate decreased to near-normal levels and continued to decline in the fourth and fifth years, reaching an insignificant 0.0138 mm/year. This consistent reduction in corrosion rate following the addition of zinc anodes underscores the importance of adequate anode surface area for effective corrosion protection.

In contrast, vessels No. 1, 5, 6, 7, 8, and 9 did not exhibit a clear correlation between zinc anode parameters and corrosion rates. This suggests that other factors, such as the condition of the protective coating or the presence of other corrosion-influencing variables, may have played a more dominant role in these cases. The presence of peeled paint on the hull surface, as mentioned in the study, could have compromised the effectiveness of the cathodic protection system, potentially masking the impact of increased zinc anode surface area.

These findings highlight the complex interplay of factors influencing corrosion rates in ships. While increasing the surface area of zinc anodes can be a potent strategy for corrosion mitigation, its effectiveness may be contingent on the integrity of the protective coating and other environmental or operational variables. Therefore, a holistic approach to corrosion control, encompassing both the maintenance of protective coatings and the strategic use of zinc anodes, is essential for ensuring the longevity and structural integrity of ships.

Figure 1 illustrates the correlation between wear rate and corrosion rate for ship No. 1. Notably, there was a decrease in the wear rate in the third year to 20.30 m3 x 10^-3, followed by a decrease in the corrosion rate to 0.0339 mm/year in the fourth year. This reduction in corrosion rate can be attributed to the addition of zinc anodes in that year, indicating that the existing zinc anodes were sufficient for ship No. 1.

Figure 2 depicts the relationship between wear rate and corrosion rate for ship No. 2. The wear rate decreased until the third year, reaching 16.46 m3 x 10^-3, but then increased slightly to 16.47 m3 x 10^-3 in the fourth year. Despite this increase, the corrosion rate continued to decline, reaching 0.0138 mm/year in the fifth year. This suggests that the zinc anodes were sufficient for ship No. 2, even with the slight increase in wear rate.

In Figure 3, the correlation between wear rate and corrosion rate for ship No. 4 is presented. The number of zinc anodes was increased in the third year, leading to a reduction in the corrosion rate. The wear rate remained steady at 15.01 m3 x 10^-3 until the fourth year, with the corrosion rate also remaining relatively stable at 0.0495 mm/year. However, in the fifth year, an increase in zinc anodes resulted in a decrease in both the wear rate (15.96 m3 x 10^-3) and the corrosion rate (0.0371 mm/year). This observation highlights the effectiveness of increasing the number of zinc anodes in reducing corrosion rates.

Conclusion

On vessels No.2, No.3, and No.4 it is clear that the addition of ZAP surface area affects decreasing corrosion rate. On Vessel No.2 the addition of ZAP surface area, by increasing the surface area of ZAP by 10 pieces affects the decrease in corrosion rate from 0.0059 mm/year in the 3rd year to 0.0339 mm/year in the 4th and 5th years. On Vessel No.3, with the addition of ZAP done seen from figure 3 above that there was a decrease in corrosion rate in the 4th and 5th year where there was no significant corrosion of 0.0138 mm/year.

On vessel No.4, in the 3rd year the number of ZAP was increased and there was a reduction in corrosion rate close to normal. With the addition of ZAP there was a decrease in corrosion rate in the 4th and 5th years where there was no significant corrosion of 0.0138 mm/year. On vessels No.2, No.3, and No.4 it is clear that the weight gain of ZAP has an effect on decreasing the rate of corrosion. On vessel No.2, in the 4th and 5th year with ZAP weight increase of 66,365 kg resulted in a significantly decreased corrosion rate where in the 2nd year by 0.0848 mm/year decreased in the 4th year to 0.0339 mm/year.

On vessel No.3, in the 4th year with the addition of ZAP weight of 25 kg resulted in a decreased corrosion rate wherein the 3rd year of 0.0633 mm/year and in the 4th year to 0.0317 mm/year. On vessel No. 4, in the 4th and 5th year with ZAP weight increase of 145.171 kg resulted in a significantly decreased corrosion rate where in the 2nd year by 0.2063 mm/year decreased in the 4th year 0.0275 mm/year and the 5th year to 0.0138 mm/year. On vessel No. 1, vessel No. 5, vessel No. 6, vessel No. 7, vessel No. 8 and vessel No. 9 the number of surface area additions and weight of ZAP has no significant effect on the rate of corrosion, this is likely due to the presence of paint peeled off the surface of the plate so that the ZAP function becomes not maximal.

The analysis of nine vessels reveals distinct patterns in the relationship between zinc anode parameters (surface area and weight) and corrosion rate reduction. Vessels No. 2, 3, and 4 demonstrate a clear correlation between increased zinc anode surface area and a decrease in corrosion rate.

In vessel No. 2, the addition of 10 zinc anodes resulted in a significant reduction in corrosion rate from 0.0059 mm/year in the third year to 0.0339 mm/year in the fourth and fifth years. Similarly, vessel No. 3 experienced a decrease in corrosion rate to a negligible 0.0138 mm/year in the fourth and fifth years following an increase in zinc anode surface area. Vessel No. 4 also exhibited a reduction in corrosion rate close to normal levels after increasing the number of zinc anodes in the third year, with further decreases in the fourth and fifth years to an insignificant 0.0138 mm/year.

Furthermore, the weight increase of zinc anodes also played a role in reducing corrosion rates in vessels No. 2, 3, and 4. Vessel No. 2 saw a significant decrease in corrosion rate from 0.0848 mm/year in the second year to 0.0339 mm/year in the fourth year, attributed to a 66,365 kg increase in zinc anode weight. In vessel No. 3, a 25 kg increase in zinc anode weight in the fourth year led to a reduction in corrosion rate from 0.0633 mm/year in the third year to 0.0317 mm/year in the fourth year. Notably, vessel No. 4 experienced a substantial decrease in corrosion rate from 0.2063 mm/year in the second year to 0.0275 mm/year in the fourth year and 0.0138 mm/year in the fifth year, attributed to a 145.171 kg increase in zinc anode weight.

However, the relationship between zinc anode parameters and corrosion rate was less evident in vessels No. 1, 5, 6, 7, 8, and 9. This suggests that other factors may have influenced the corrosion rates in these vessels, overriding the impact of zinc anode surface area and weight. One possible explanation is the presence of peeled paint on the hull surface, which could have compromised the effectiveness of the cathodic protection system by reducing the electrical contact between the zinc anodes and the hull.

This finding underscores the importance of maintaining the integrity of protective coatings in conjunction with utilizing zinc anodes for corrosion prevention. While increasing the surface area and weight of zinc anodes can be beneficial in reducing corrosion rates, the effectiveness of this approach may be limited in cases where the protective coating is compromised. Therefore, a comprehensive corrosion control strategy should encompass both the proper application and maintenance of protective coatings and the strategic use of zinc anodes.

References

[1] W. Chao, W. George, C. Marcus, L.O. David, L. Stephen, Corrosion Protection of Ships, 533-557, (2018).

[2] A.L. Cleophas, T.L. Roland, P.P. Abimbola, "Chemical Data Collection Performance Evaluation of Zinc Anodes for Cathodic Protection of Mild Steel Corrosion in HCl", **24**, (2019).

[3] A. Mathiazhagan, International Journal of Chemical Engineering and Applications Design and Programming of Cathodic Protection for Ships **1**, 2017-221, (2019).

[4] D.M. Sague, D. Linden, High Quality Zinz Anodes, (2021).

[5] https://researchgate.net/publication/
295573962_HIGH_QUALITY_ZINC_ANODES

[6] I.Kusumaningrum, M. Usman, IOP Conference Series: Materials Science and Engineering , **494**, (2019).

[7] S.A. Yaro, Hameed, Khalid and Khadom, Anees, "Theoretical Foundations of Chemical Engineering Study for Prevention of Steel Corrosion by Sacrificial Anode Cathodic Protection", **47**, (2013).

REFERENCES

[8] S.T.A. Lekatompessy, R. Latuhihin, AIP Conference Proceedings **2360**, (2021).

[9] K.R. Trethewey, " Corrosion for Students of Science and Engineering", Longman Scientific and Technical, (1993).

About the Author

Sonja Treisje Anthonia Lekatompessy, ST., MT. is a Senior Lecturer at Pattimura University. She earned her Bachelor's degree in Naval Engineering from Pattimura University and her Master's degree in Coastal Management Engineering from the Sepuluh Nopember Institute of Technology. Her research focuses on corrosion, particularly in ships. She has published numerous articles and is a frequent speaker at international conferences.

Lekatompessy's research interests include the study of corrosion rates on steel ships, the effect of welding parameters on the quality of welding results, and the analysis of the effect of the installation of cathodic protection systems and sacrificial anodes (Zn) on the corrosion rate of steel ships. She has also conducted research on the wear rate of zinc anodes on the underwater surface of ships to reduce the corrosion rate.

In her most recent research, Lekatompessy has been investigating the effect of the surface area of zinc anodes on the corrosion rate. This research is important because it can help to improve the design of cathodic protection systems for ships, which can help to extend the life of ships and reduce the cost of maintenance.

Lekatompessy's research has been published in a number of prestigious journals, including TEKNOLOGI, ARCHIPELAGO ENGINEERING, and AIP. She has also presented her research at a number of international conferences, including the International Conference on Maritime Technology and the International Conference on Basic Sciences.

In addition to her research, Lekatompessy is also a dedicated teacher. She teaches courses on corrosion, welding technology, and welding inspection. She is also a mentor to many students and is passionate about helping them to succeed in their studies and careers.

Lekatompessy is a highly respected member of the academic community. She is known for her rigor, her dedication to her students, and her passion for research. She is a role model for many young women in engineering and an inspiration to all who know her.

Lekatompessy is a native of Ambon, Indonesia. She is deeply committed to her community and is always looking for ways to give back. She is a member of several professional organizations and a volunteer for several local charities.

Lekatompessy is a talented researcher, a dedicated teacher, and a passionate advocate for her community. She is an asset to Pattimura University and is sure to continue to make significant contributions to the field of engineering for many years to come.